An Introdu
Working W
Fathers

by Tony Ivens and Nick Clements

First published in Great Britain by
Fatherskills Publishers, 2005

ISBN: 0-9551725-0-0

Published by:
Fatherskills
Ty Mawr
Llanllwch
Carmarthen SA31 3RN
www.fatherskills.co.uk

Illustrated by:
Sophie Cobb   e-mail: sophiecobb@fsmail.net
www. valleyandvale.co.uk

Contents

Acknowledgements

We would like to acknowledge that this book is a direct result of the combined thirty years work undertaken by both of us in Wales. The expertise we have accumulated has been through working with thousands of people during that time; many of whom have been challenging in their behaviour, coming from a diversity of backgrounds, and enabling us to experiment, explore new projects, and develop the theories in this book.

During those years we have been employed by a range of organisations, including Local Authorities, Government Departments, Universities and Colleges, and Voluntary Sector organisations. We have also lectured and given workshops to those interested in our work throughout Britain, America, Germany, and India.

We would like to thank Alex Bowen at Valley and Vale for her support and encouragement. Sue Marsden from NCH Cymru for the opportunity to set us on this path. Sophie Cobb for creating the illustrations.

Finally, both of us would like to take this opportunity to thank our own children for showing us the mistakes we have made, and probably will continue to make!

FATHERSKILLS

This book accompanies the training programme of the same name run by Fatherskills. We are a partnership set up by two experienced and professional practitioners with over 30 years experience of working in the social, care and arts fields. We are acknowledged as the leading practitioners in Wales for working with fathers and men, and we provide a wide range of training, consultancies and workshops for professionals in care, health, social and youth services.

We offer a comprehensive service of consultations, workshops, talks, mentoring and training. These are suitable for professionals who work with fathers and men. They come from our belief that all such activities must be child-centred, and should have the welfare and well being of the children as their main aim.

All our training programmes and workshops come from our own personal experiences, from our work in a variety of social and cultural settings, and from the wide ranging experiences we have in group work, one to one, and counselling. Both of us have specialised in working with men and father for many years, and we know the ways in which to engage fathers with their children, and the particular needs of men in such circumstances.

The following is some of the feedback from professionals who have attended Fatherskills training:-

* *It made me realise how important it is to have the father involved in the child's life.*

* *The course was of great practical value and has left me with a ' tool' that can be used.*

* *As I am so new at my job, I found everything useful.*

* *Fatherhood being reaffirmed.*

* *Has provided me with the opportunity to facilitate to other co-workers in order to set up groups in our local community.*

* *All the contents were excellent and delivered very professionally.*

* *I feel this is a very user friendly programme with exercises which provide good visual aids to learning that is well structured.*

* *I believe the entire course was useful.*

* *Consolidated knowledge. Well organised and useful training resource.*

Men in general desire what is good, not merely what their fathers had.

Aristotle(384BC - 322BC): *Politics*

Introduction

This book is for professionals working with fathers and father figures, and is produced by two fathers who have a great deal of experience and knowledge, not only from bringing up their own children, but also from working in this field for over 30 years.

Parenting is an immensely difficult, complex and transformative experience, it is probably the most important thing anyone can do. It will last a lifetime and most other jobs pale into insignificance alongside it. Parenting can be the most fulfilling, loving and liberating experience, as well being the most challenging and personally stressful time, it may leave us vulnerable, perplexed and angry, but it will always be worthwhile.

We all acknowledge parenting is best undertaken as a couple, and when this couple is a man and woman they bring a wide range of inputs, differing perspectives, complex conscious and unconscious triggers, behavioural patterns, and learnt experiences to the task. Even when these two are loving and supportive to each other and their children, it is still a fraught and stressful experience, often they need support from extended families, relatives and care professionals.

The men in this equation need support and encouragement. All children have a biological father and have father figures in their lives. Many fathers don't have access to their children for many different reasons, many feel inadequate and unable to cope. But, the majority of them are doing vital work, still learning and being available for their children. Due to a variety of reasons, these really important individuals are often ignored, sidelined and not consulted when it comes to parenting their children. There has been very little promotion of positive parenting for fathers, mothers have been expected and given a huge responsibility, which they have often found intolerable. This situation needs to be changed.

This programme promotes ways of including fathers in the services being offered to parents, and will encourage the professionals to think creatively about how they can include fathers in the future.

Chapter One:
Values

Working with fathers

Aims

*   To explain the principles and practice of working with dads

*   To examine best practice within organisations

*   Offering practical suggestions for recruiting fathers

*   To support dads to play and interact with their children

*   To challenge our own attitudes to bringing up children

*   To examine the differences between the ways that fathers

       and mothers parent their children

*   To provide the skills necessary to facilitate a

       meaningful relationship between father and child.

Outcomes

*   Understanding barriers to involvement with children

*   Increased confidence in the father's parenting role

*   Higher outcomes for children

*   Improved relationships between partners

*   Increased age appropriate play with children

*   Develops meaningful communication between fathers

       and children.

Positive Parenting

Parenting is easiest when it is based on good communications. This works both ways. Children have the right to express themselves, learn and develop. But parents also have the right to set limits about which behaviours are acceptable and which are not.

Key aspects include: -

* Showing appreciation and attention as ways of increasing positive behaviours.

* Recognising children's developmental abilities.

* Balancing power between parents and children.

* Acknowledging Children's Rights as laid out in the UN Convention of the Rights of the Child.

Please, remember, there is no such thing as a perfect parent!

Aims of Positive Parenting

To reduce problem behaviours in our children.

*   Find ways to encourage them to listen, and comply with what they're told.
*   Decrease challenging behaviour.
*   Manage temper tantrums and other aggressive behaviours.

To help children gain new social and emotional skills, and to develop these both at home and in school.

*   Increase their ability to interact successfully with the world around them.
*   Increase children's understanding of their feelings.
*   Increase their ability to problem solve.
*   Help them to control some of the more excessive behaviours. Learn how to co-operate both in and outside the home.
*   Encourage their ability to share and recognise the needs of others.

To provide parents with the skills they need to manage and nurture their children.

* Improve communication skills.

* To recognise the importance of praise and positive feedback.

* To reduce the use of criticisms and unnecessary commands.

* Learning when to ignore behaviours.

* Set effective rules and boundaries, along with the appropriate consequences.

* To be consistent.

* Replace smacking and other physical punishments with other non-violent alternatives.

* Improve problem solving skills and anger management.

* Increase family support networks.

And finally we need to remember, being a parent (irrespective of gender) is probably the most important thing any of us will be asked to do, yet nobody teaches us how to do it!

Child Centred

Although Positive Parenting seeks to address the needs of both children and parents, we should nevertheless always recognise that the needs of the child are paramount. This is laid down in statute (Children Act 1989), and should underpin all our work.

With this in mind,

* Our work with Fathers should always seek to improve the quality of life for their child.

* The needs of the child should come first.

* We should support children's rights as laid out in the United Nations Convention on the Rights of the Child (UNCRC)

The UNCRC states : -

Article 3. *"All organisations concerned with children should work towards what is best for each child".*

Artilcle 9. *"children should not be separated from their parents unless it is for their own good............ Children whose parents have separated have the right to stay in contact with both parents, unless this might hurt the child"*

Article 18. *"Both parents share responsibility for bringing up their children. Governments should help parents by providing services to support them........."*

Some Current Thinking on Parenting

The Welsh Assembly Government believes that smacking children is wrong. We do not think it encourages adults, children and young peope to respect each other. We believe that there are better ways of dealing with difficult behaviour and teaching children right from wrong.

In the proposed Parenting Action Plan for Wales, the Assembly states:-

"The direction for developing parenting support provided through this plan will seek to address the needs of all parents, and to cover parenting support for different groups of children andyoung people. It recognises the needs of mothers and fathers, of male and female carers, are not always the same."

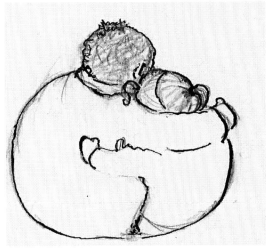

Chapter Two:
Rationale

Why We Should Work With Fathers

Over the past ten years, all UK social and care agencies have become increasingly aware of a huge need in our society. It begins with a lack of father's involvement in pre and ante-natal care; absentee fathers; the low esteem and low academic achievement levels of boys; the anti-social and damaging behaviour of teenagers; and the lack of good male role models. These are complex and difficult issues, each family is different and each case needs care and attention. However, we know that these issues need to be addressed as a matter of urgency, and that solutions and ways of working with fathers need to be found.

Here are just some of the well researched reasons for doing so: -

* Nearly a third of all childcare in the UK today is carried out by men! *(Pleck & Mascaidrelli. 2004)*

* All children need and benefit from a positive male role model.

* Involvement from fathers is a predictor of higher academic achievement. *(Scott. 2004)*

* Children with involved fathers are less likely to engage in offending behaviour. *(Beail & McGuire. 1997)*

* Around a half of all Parenting Orders are issued to single parent. *(Ghate & Ramella. 2002)*

* Fathers are more likely to be employed, and therefore less able to spend more time with their children. *(EOC. 2003)*

* Numerous studies have demonstrated that the vast majority of men in the UK today would welcome the opportunity to be more involved with their children. *(EOC. 2005)*

* Expectant fathers may, like their partners, experience hormonal changes.Prolactin (promotes lactation and fostering behaviour) increases by 20% on average during the 3 weeks before birth. also, at the time of birth,men's testostorone levels can drop dramatically by up to 33%. *(Storey. 2000)*

* One of the best predictors of a mothers success at breastfeeding is her perception of her partner's support. *(Whelan & Lupton. 1998)*

* UK breastfeeding rates are very low – only 28% of mothers will still be breastfeeding after 4 months.

* Pre-school children were found to be more sociable starting nursery school, when they had spent time playing with their fathers. *(Lewis. 1997)*

* Traditional parenting support services have been targeted at mothers.

* There is now clear evidence that in dual earner families where mothers work full time in the first year of children's life, increased father involvement can compensate or 'protect' children from experiencing less overall parental time. *(Goldman. 2005)*

* The proportion of children living in lone mother households increased from 11 per cent in 1981 to 21 per cent of households with dependant children by 2001. the proportion of lone father households has remained stable at 2 per cent throughout this period. *(Collingwood et al. 2004)*

* The qualities of the new model father are; presence, involvement, putting children's needs first, approachability, nurturing and caring. *(Henwood & Procter. 2003)*

Father Figures

Within this work language and the use of words is very important. In order for us to be as inclusive as possible, we use the phrase 'father figure'.

What is a father figure?
A wide range of men take this role on, and they may well not have any biological connections to the child involved.

They include:-

* Biological fathers
* Step fathers
* Partners to a mother
* Grandfathers
* Elder brothers
* Uncles
* Men living in shared accommodation

All these different men can be seen by a child as a 'father figure' given a particular set of circumstances, and often the smallest details of their behaviour are being watched, copied and examined during every day of contact by that child. The father figure may well not want to be seen as such, but because of close proximity, it is happening anyway, whether they like it or not. Certainly,

if the father is not present, and no man has taken his place, the next best thing will be taken by the child. Step-fathers and other similar roles are very difficult to take on, such individuals can find the work involved in caring for a child very onerous, and they can become de-motivated if not supported and encouraged. The rewards are the same for any of these individuals, but the fact that they are not the biological father may play a major factor. Our present society is full of examples of fathers who are doing a wonderful job by sticking it out, and almost an equal number of men who have given up and now have no contact, or only very limited contact, with the child. Even with limited access the man is still a father figure, and is a role model for the child, and the examples of behaviour will be used in the future.

For those who are consciously taking on this role, there are a wide range of motivations, and these will affect how they interact with the child. The motivation for many father figures is from the child's perspective - *"I want to do this for my children".* First time fathers are often in shock, hugely impacted upon by the advent of this new arrival, and they need to find justifications for staying during these often stressful early times. Whatever the motivation, by spending time with the child and expending energy and effort, the man will be influencing and affecting the child profoundly.

The father figure needs to be just that, a 'father' figure, not a copy of a mother. The father provides similar and very complimentary inputs to the child, but they are separate and vitally important for the healthy development of the child. The father can perform all the tasks that the mother does, except for breast feeding, and is capable of taking on the full time role of carer. However, there are many subtle differences in the ways that a father does things as compared to a mother.

The simplest task for a father is to provide safety and comfort for the child, and the easiest way to impart this is to give the child a cuddle. A father's cuddle is different to a mother's, and the effects of having a cuddle with a father figure are different for the child. Such subtle differences are too often ignored, or not even considered, and it is only when we examine our own childhood objectively that we can start to see these delicate and subtle differences.

A father supplies a wide range of experiences to the child which are vital in the development of a whole and healthy adult. The father's behaviour needs to be in keeping with his strengths, skills and abilities, and not restricted. He must be able to express how he wants to do things with the child, and be able to explore them fully. Rough and tumble play is an example of this kind of behaviour.

Michael Durham   Sunday Times, March 2003

"Fathers who play-fight with their children are helping them grow into well-adjusted adults. The tendency of men to rough-house and be physical with youngsters has been discouraged since the 1960's, when child psychologists suggested it might be harmful.

Now the first rigorous study of the issue has shown that children with such fathers are among the friendliest and most peaceful and popular in the school playground. By contrast, children who are mollycoddled at home and discouraged from rough behaviour are much more likely to turn into bullies or their victims. Charlie Lewis, professor of development psychology at Lancaster University and an authority on child-father relationships, said. "There is something special about rough-house play with dads that helps a child to learn self-control.

Such findings will appear counter-intuitive to mothers, many of whom assume that simulated violence and toys such as plastic guns and swords will predispose their children to violence. Such fears are misplaced. Mothers should instead let children and fathers act out their aggression in a friendly and controlled way. It forces a child to confront how he or she relates to other people and it's a safe place to learn the rules of engagement."

Gender Roles

We all assume, in this modern day and age, that the divide between the gender roles in the family and at home have changed from those of fifty years ago *(Allen & Hawkins. 1999)*. In order to test this, in 2004, we asked a group of year nine students at Bryngwyn Comprehensive School in Llanelli, what are the roles that their mothers and fathers take on?

These are their responses:-

FATHER	MOTHER
Control the children	Having kids
Keeping children safe	Cooking
Teaching right from wrong	Keeping the house tidy
Money	Bringing up children
Getting Jobs	Taking kids to school
Discipline	Pocket money
Embarrassing the children	Being strict
Teaching respect/trust	Teaching about emotions
Taking the children on treats	Buying the clothes
Being lazy	Being busy
Watching telly	

The Deficit Perspective

"All too often fathers are seen as part of the problem, and not part of the solution".

The traditional gender stereotyping of roles has resulted in men more often being seen as part of the problem, rather than part of the solution. Domestic violence cases and instances of child abuse are often (rightly) laid at the door of men. However this by no means validates the view that all men behave in this way. If we make the comparison with something like racism, we all agree that it is no longer acceptable to pre-judge an individual simply on the colour of their skin, yet we are still guilty of making these kinds of assumptions when it comes to men and their relationship with children.

The father who was challenged because he was sitting on a park bench watching some children play (in reality they were his own children), vividly illustrates this point. No one would think of challenging a women in this situation, yet because he was a male, the suspicion existed that in some way he was up to no good.

Until this kind of cultural perception about who men are is challenged, we are unlikely to encourage more men to take an active role in raising their children.

The following are some of the most common scenarios where this way of thinking is likely to be encountered: -

*   Child protection cases

*   Invisible fathers

*   Domestic violence

*   Substance abuse

*   Relationships with schools

*   Authoritarian / dominating fathers

We are all conscious as professionals of the potential dangers of labelling children, however all too often we fail to transfer these principles to our work with men.

There are already deeply ingrained cultural prejudices around men and young children (see section on discrimination), we need to be taking a lead on challenging these perceptions, not reinforcing them!

Father Friendly Policies

Working with fathers begins with the way that, as an organisation, professionals think about fathers in the overall planning of their services. If fathers are to be engaged with successfully, it can only happen when the whole ethos of the team includes them at the strategic level *(O'Brien. 2004).*

As well as supporting and encouraging more men to take a greater role in bringing up their children, we also need to be challenging the policies within our own organisations with regard to male recruitment. We are not suggesting that discrimination exists, the issues are far more complex than that, but the figures speak for themselves.

Childcare Professions by Gender UK 2001

OCCUPATION	MALE	FEMALE	MALE%
NURSERY NURSES	1,430	136,220	1.0%
CHILDMINDERS & RELATED	2,610	116.010	2.2%
PLAYGROUP WORKERS	3,570	58,410	5.8%

Within the context of this kind of data, it should come as no surprise to realise that many men see themselves as marginalised when entering the childcare professions. Even when projects do employ a dedicated worker to engage with fathers, these individuals often report that they feel unsupported in their role and that the reason they have been appointed has more to do with ticking all the right boxes than to do with engaging with fathers at all levels of service delivery.

A common scenario is that having appointed a "fathers worker", any and all referrals relating to men's issues will arrive on their desk, irrespective of the workers training or skill levels. We would not presume to follow this model with parenting support for mothers, but see no incongruity in doing it with fathers .

Father workers are often expected to be a jack of all trades with the result that they can feel inadequate and unsupported in their role.

The following is a typical list of questions that any organisation hoping to successfully engage with fathers should be asking themselves.

* Do you have a long term commitment to the work? Results rarely come overnight.

* Have ALL members of staff received appropriate training for working with fathers?

* Does your project have clear targets for engaging fathers?

* Are staff kept up to date with the latest developments and research on working with men?

* Is the project committed to increasing the number of male workers it employs? Do you have targets for this?

* Is your practice always carried out in "male friendly" environments?

* Does your monitoring, evaluation and assessments ALWAYS include talking to the fathers? Even when the father is no longer resident in the family home they still remain the child's father.

* When conducting consultation and participation exercises do you ALWAYS include fathers in this process?

* Is your approach tokenistic?

* Do you promote the importance of the role of fathers when involved in multi-agency working?

* Are the images you use in your publicity material and literature inclusive?

* Do you make conscious efforts to avoid the deficit perspective?

Male Staff in Caring Professions

When the care professions start to deal with men and fathers there can be problems in terms of language, prejudices and trust. One of the factors in this equation is the chronic lack of male staff in the caring professions. This has been the case for many years, and will not change overnight, it is embedded in the services, it reflects the low esteem that such jobs carry, and the lack of understanding of their value within the wider community.

We recognise that this is a principle, an ideal. However, it is essential that the caring professions realises the lack of male staff is a major issue, and start down the road towards addressing and re-balancing their recruitment. It is impossible and undesirable to have an all-male staff, but the present balance is not good, and will continue to discourage fathers and men from participating in the services.

This is not to say that men are better in this job. The vast majority of women are very good at their jobs - they are aware of the fathers, and encourage and support them. It is a difficult enough job in the first place, and we recognise that the vast majority of workers are providing a fantastically effective service. However, it is a simple fact that a father would feel safer and more at ease with a male professional *(Heubeck et al. 1986)*. If we reverse the roles and we were to set up a meeting to discuss sensitive female issues with a mother, and the person to do the work is a man, there would instantly be objections and people questioning the validity of the work.

The advantages of having a larger number of male staff are instantly recognisable and worthwhile:-

* It will encourage more fathers and men to partici-pate and be part of their children's future.
* It will have a positive effect on the mothers as well, it will encourage them to discuss issues with their partners, support them in their attempts to increase the participation of the father figure, which so many mothers are presently seeking.
* It will encourage fathers to remain in contact with their children for longer, and enable them to take child care and support matters more seriously.
* It will decrease the numbers of attacks on staff.
* It will be a factor in the development of better and more cohesive services which will hopefully become less of a burden on the local authorities of the future.

Fathers and Education

Research nowadays clearly demonstrates that "what parents do with their children at home, is far more important to their eventual   achievement in life than their social class or level of education" *(Goldman. 2005)*. The problem lies with   the use of the gender neutral term 'parent'. Within the parameters of the traditional gender stereotyping of roles, home learning was nearly always seen as part of the mothers role. However this is starting to change, questions around science, maths, computers and much of the IT field is now seen as something which is the responsibility of the father. The reverse would also seem to be true, with mothers taking a more active role when it comes to supporting their children in sporting activities.

It is now generally recognised that it is better for children to have more than one active carer or parent *(Dunn et al. 2000)*. Indeed some psychologists talk about a 'double dose' *(Jaffee et al. 2003)* effect in which children are influenced (both positively and negatively) by the active involvement of two parents or carers and the interactions between them.

Rebecca Goldman's *"Fathers' Involvement in their Children's Education"* (NFPI 2005) meta-analysis of a number of high quality studies concludes that:-

* There is consistent evidence that the quality and content of fathers' involvement (in their children's learning) matter much more for children's outcomes than the quantity of time that a father and child are in contact or the frequency of contact or visits. This applies to both resident and non-resident parents.

* In particular, fathers' affection, support and 'authoritative' parenting style are related to children's positive educational outcomes. Poor parenting by fathers is associated with children's decreased educational attainment.

* It is important for teachers to find out about fathers' involvement in the lives of the children in their class so that they can understand the successes and problems of these children much better, and work with these children in a more appropriate way.

* The studies show that fathers' greater interest and involvement in their children's learning and in schools are statistically associated with better educational outcomes for children, including better exam results, better school attendance and behaviour, and higher educational expectations. There are also associations with better social and emotional outcomes for children.

* In one study, a father's interest in his child's education had a stronger association with the likelihood of that child having qualifications in adult life than did contact with police, poverty, family type or the child's personality.

* These statistical associations with fathers' involvement are independent of mothers' involvement . They exist for primary school children and secondary school children; for children in two parent families, single-mother families with non-resident fathers, and single-father families; and are irrespective of the gender of the child.

* Mothers' involvement is no substitute for fathers' involvement.

* There are however mixed findings on any differences of the strengths of impacts of fathers' involvement and mothers' involvement. There are also mixed findings on whether or not the strength of impact of fathers' involvement is greater for boys than girls.

Fathers are more likely to be involved in their child's learning when:-

* the child's mother is involved in the child's learning and education

* the father is resident with the child

* there are good relations between the father and the mother, especially in situations where the father is non-resident

* there has been earlier (post-natal/pre-school/primary school) involvement by the father

* the father and the mother have higher qualification levels
* the child is in primary school rather than secondary school (which also holds for mothers' involvement in education)
* the father comprises a 'father only household' (lone father).

We also need to be clear when talking about learning that we should not be restricting ourselves simply to academic knowledge. Children need to learn life skills, this is particularly relevant for boys who need a positive role model. There can be hidden dangers in this, for example, if the parent reading at home (either on their own or with a child) is more often the mother than the father, this can lead to boys thinking that reading (and perhaps learning generally) is a female activity.

Support

We tend to use the word 'support' an awful lot, not only in respect of working with fathers, but also in terms of families generally. It is probably worth taking a few moments to examine what we mean, or should mean, when we talk about support. Broadly speaking, support sub-divides into two categories, formal and informal.

However in both categories a number of key elements should be present which will mean the difference between success and failure. The following, well quoted, service user definition of support illustrates this point.

"..support means that you are still in charge; the parent is still in charge and you are just asking for help, advice and whatever but you are the one in charge. You are not handing over....your kids to someone else to take over. You are still in charge of them" Mother, lone parent, low income, sick child. (PRB. 2004)

In addition to the need for fathers (and parents generally) to stay in control, we should also recognise that it is generally they, the father or parent who knows more about the child than us, the professionals. They are the experts when it comes to their family. Our task is to direct that expertise in such a way as to benefit the child.

This can only happen as a result of seeing support as a relationship. The rules for this are no different than any other relationship, the more you put in, the more you can get out!

These relationships however can become difficult when the need arises to refer to other services. Fathers are no different to anyone else, they find it easier to develop a relationship with an individual than with an organisation. Whenever possible we should strive to maintain as much continuity as possible.

This leads us to the final element regarding support, it needs to be seen as a process rather than a list of events. Not only will the relationship change over time, but also the circumstances surrounding a father and his family inevitably change. This is often in no way related to the input that we as professionals are providing. Unless we are aware of these changes, we run the risk of this input becoming irrelevant.

Chapter Three:
Inclusion

Joined up Thinking/Services

In an ideal world there would not have to be a need to stress joined up thinking in terms of parenting services, but all too often a service provider contradicts or duplicates the work of another. This can deter and frustrate the parents involved, adding to the tensions and prejudices already held by those individuals, fathers can be particularly prone to this. In order to counteract this, we would seek the following;-

Early intervention -
Many fathers find the early stages of parenthood alienating, difficult and confusing, as so many of them say, *"a baby doesn't come with a manual"*. If a father can be encouraged, made to feel part of the process, made to feel wanted by the professionals involved, it would have a positive knock on effect for the child. It will encourage them to continue to participate in the upbringing of the child, and enable them to feel confident about their role and responsibilities. This can only be a good thing.

Normalise the role -
We need to see professionals being aware of the father, and it being standard practice for them to encourage him to participate in the child's upbringing. It would be a very positive step if these professionals were to ask him

questions, include him in discussions, ask his opinion. This would have a very positive effect on the father, and would also give the mother the feeling that she is being supported by the father. The only way we can encourage such inclusive experiences is to look at these elements being included in the basic training for workers in this field.

Include fathers in the whole range of support -
All too often professionals don't include the father in vitally important discussions, even though his is actually in the room. Many fathers talk of how invisible they feel when the health visitor comes, and they will often go out of the room and exclude themselves. This is not a good thing. We all need to encourage them to feel part of the developmental process of their child, and that their views and feelings are worth considering. This feeling of being invisible starts when the baby is born, and can continue right they way through the child's development.

Joined up Services Need to Include:-

Midwives	Health visitors
Surestart	Primary schools
Secondary education	Youth Justice
Parent support programmes	

Discrimination

In 2005 we undertook an exercise with a group of fathers in Mountain Ash, to examine the forms of discrimination which they had encountered since becoming fathers.

Health visitors and other professionals

They commented on how invisible they felt, how ignored and unwanted they were made to feel. Another major factor here was the language barrier, they felt that things were not being explained very easily, and the language used was a barrier to their clear understanding of the situation. This was a major factor for the mothers as well.

Mother and baby changing rooms

They had found that these were often situated in the Women's Toilets, and there had been a variety of problems in terms of gaining access to the facilities, and the lack of understanding of staff.

Shopping centres

They all told of experiences of shop assistants surprise and suspicion when they were out buying, particularly, their daughters, and their sons, clothes. This applied in terms of buying nappies and other baby accessories.

Mother and toddler groups

Most had experienced so much embarrassment and dis-comfort that they had not persisted in going. Feelings of being judged, being watched, being an outsider, along with the alienating environment, mother and woman friendly, but not welcoming for a man. Those that had persisted in going, had sustained their participation through a jovial and boisterous presence, but this was an effort, and they all had to prepare themselves for the task.

Parks

The simple experience of taking their children out to the park to play, had now become a difficult and often em-barrassing event. By simply sitting on a park bench and watching the children they became the target of suspi-cion from mothers, and openly hostile responses from park wardens.

School

Waiting outside for your child, had like the park, become fraught and alienating. Many had been confronted by school officials, and all felt that the other mothers viewed them with suspicion and prejudice.

How Family Centres are Working with Fathers

A report titled 'Fathers and family centres: engaging fathers in preventative services *(Ghate et al. 2000)*.

The report examined what helps and hinders fathers' involvement with family centres. The research found:

* Family centres are still strongly female dominated. However, many centres are actively trying to work with fathers, enjoying varying degrees of success.

* The type of centre mattered less than the general 'orientation' to working with men. Having some identifiable strategy for working with fathers mattered more than what the strategy was.

* While family centres cater relatively well to fathers in non-typical circumstances (e.g. to lone fathers or fathers with a particularly high level of involvement in childcare), centres were less successful at engaging with other, more 'ordinary' fathers.

*   Fathers often found the activities offered at family centres, such as crafts and alternative therapies, unappealing and 'unmanly'. They preferred more active and practically focused things to do, such as outdoor activities and DIY.

*   Centres often take a different approach depending on the sex of the parent. Work with the women tends to follow a family-focused model in which women's needs as mother, and as a woman in their own right, are acknowledged. On the other hand, work with fathers tends to be more child-focused, with an emphasis on childcare and little that caters to fathers' other, wider interests.

*   The research concluded there is a need for greater clarity about whom family centres are intended to serve. To work successfully with fathers, centres need to consider working with fathers as men, not just as child carers.

Chapter Four:
Recruitment

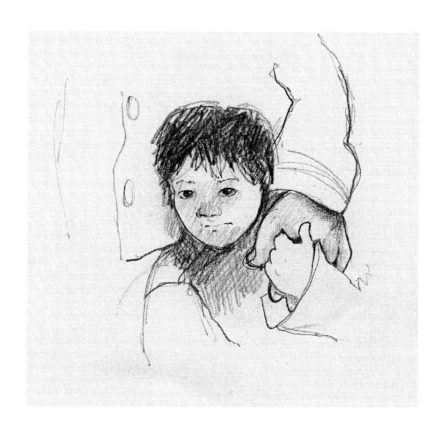

Male Role Models

The statistics in terms of the numbers of single parent families, and the numbers of children who have no contact with their fathers, are increasing each year.

This has a major effect on all of those involved, and is a determining factor in a wide range of social changes. The effects are seen in:

*   low academic achievement levels of boys in school
*   teenage crime
*   lack of respect being shown by young people

It is not the only factor at play here, but it is part of an overall picture of decline, and it is now a high priority on government and local authority agendas.

If we are to do something about this, we need to know a little more about what is special about the father/child relationship, and particularly the father/son relationship.

*   A father gives a different dimension to the learning experience of children, he provides a similar but different way of being, particularly learning.

*   He teaches through action. The father does not necessarily explain things verbally, he tends to just do things and to teach through experience.

*   This is a vital lesson for all children, but most especially boys, they will learn very quickly this way, and are able to pick up lessons efficiently by being alongside their father, watching what he is doing.

When the father is not present, then the children will learn from whoever is available, and when no father figure is present, they will have to learn from the mother and other women. This is not a bad thing, but it is an unbalanced experience. Children will naturally seek male role models, and they will make the most unlikely choices in terms of who they choose to be their role model. In a fatherless family the younger children may fixate on the oldest son. It all depends on who is around, and the ways in which such contact is maintained.

The professionals who work with single parent families need to be aware of this, it is a need within the children, and it will be playing out within the family dynamic at all times. If it is not addressed or recognised, it can cause extreme dysfunctional behaviour, and create major problems in later life *(pers obs)*. The professionals need to be able to discuss this with the mother, and to be able to support the male role models who come into the child's life. In the early years of a child's life this issue is not easily recognised or diagnosed, but it certainly becomes very apparent as the child reaches teenage years.

All too often teenagers are seeking role models, ways of being, and the only ones available are their immediate peers. When teenagers attempt to 'initiate themselves into adulthood', we almost invariably encounter anti-social and addictive behaviour. A father's role at this time is crucial, and if there is a good male role model around, who the teenager trusts, then a great deal of this can be dealt with and accommodated. When the father is not present the child will choose another to perform this role, on occasions this can be the male professionals who are there to facilitate and assist the families. It can become part of the job for these men to become male role models for the children in their care, and it is a very useful role to undertake.

Recruitment

If there is one single issue that projects struggle with more than any other, then this is it! However, approached properly, it should not in any way be insurmountable. Probably the most single important thing to bear in mind is *'be patient and stay with it'*! There will not be a queue of dads outside your door the day after you announce your service – but that does not mean that you will fail. The reason which more than any other gets in the way, is a lack of a clear idea of what you expect to achieve. Be very clear, and up front about what you are offering. Do your homework first; projects which try to impose their existing agenda onto fathers often struggle.

The 6 R's which apply to other parenting support services are equally applicable to fathers.

Services should be: -

1. Reachable: - in terms of time and place
2. Recognise:- local need
3. Respond:- to that need
4. Respect:- the different contribution which fathers offer their children
5. Refer:- on to other services when appropriate – know your limitations
6. Review:- what you are offering – don't be afraid to change things which are not working

Groupwork

Traditionally parenting programmes have invariably been run as pieces of groupwork – and there are very good reasons for having done this. However, when it comes to working with fathers this is probably the hardest way to start doing it!

   *   Men generally do not 'do groups' unless they are specifically task orientated, and even then they are often selective about which tasks they feel comfortable with.

   *   There are well identified cultural and psychological reasons why this is so; to ask men to attend a group about a task with which they are already unclear about is a double whammy!

   *   This is not to say however that it is impossible to run father's groups. Many exist, often very successfully, remember you need to walk before you can run.

   *   By far the easiest way to establish a group is to recruit from fathers with whom you have already been working

and with whom a level of basic trust has already been established.

*   Running a fathers group should be seen as a separate piece of work, and facilitators trained accordingly.

*   It is with that in mind that this programme offers a variety of meaningful ways to engage with fathers which do not involve groupwork .

Having got that out of the way – back to recruitment

Projects generally receive referrals from a variety of referrers, eg Health visitors, Social Services, schools etc etc. Talk to these people first! Find out why they would refer fathers to you, explain what you can offer, and then tailor a service to meet the need.

In addition there are almost certainly going to be existing groups attracting mothers, talk to them too, remember working with fathers has as much to offer mothers as it does to the fathers.

The biggest single reason why men will be willing to engage is when they are convinced that they are doing it for the benefit of their children (and not themselves). The vast majority of men, when asked, say that they would like to be more involved with their children!

Having got this far you will then need to identify the barriers which may be getting in the way of this happening. This most common single reason given by men when surveyed about this issue is work *(Henwood & Procter. 2003)*. You will need to be creative and imaginative about how you try to overcome this.

 Other reasons may be varied and often specific to a particular community, but some of the most common reasons are;
*   issues around transport
*   choice of venues
*   childcare
*   self esteem
*   peer group pressure
*   gender stereotyping
*   cultural or family pressures

And finally remember that women are often the gatekeepers to parenting *(Goldman. 2005)*, it is not uncommon for mothers to feel threatened (no matter what they may say to the contrary) by what they may see as an invasion of 'their territory'.

Top Ten Tips For Recruiting Dads

1. Be clear, upfront and honest about what you are offering.

2. Make sure they understand that you are not trying to turn them into mums!

3. Stress the benefits to the child or children.

4. Whenever and wherever possible, use male workers to recruit.

5. Routinely include men in your existing home visits / services.

6. Use language and images that are male friendly.

7. Recruit from as large a variety of sources as possible.

8. Word of mouth is often the most successful medium for recruitment.

9. Normalise the role.

10. Use other existing fathers to spread the word.

Chapter Five:
Methods

Strategies for Engaging

Moving forward from the assumption that groupwork is not the easiest starting point when working with Dads, we need to identify ways of encouraging and supporting fathers to develop a more meaningful relationship with their children. This should not be difficult, provided we acknowledge that not all families are the same. Fathers come in a variety of shapes and sizes, the concept of the 'generic dad' does not in reality exist.

These can include:-

*   Biological fathers
*   Single parent fathers
*   Stepfathers
*   Working fathers
*   Absent fathers
*   Grandfathers
*   Elder siblings or other family members who take on the role, eg uncles etc.
*   Separated fathers with little if any contact
*   Foster parents
*   Etc, etc.

In addition, children also come in a variety of shapes and sizes. The opportunities for spending time with a child vary enormously according to the age / stage of development of that child and their family circumstances.

Successive pieces of research have demonstrated that it is not the quantity of time spent with the child which is important, but the quality.

All of this should hopefully lead us to the recognition that we are going to need a variety of strategies when we set out to support fathers in having a more meaningful relationship with their children.

The following are a number of tried and tested ways that we can encourage and support fathers to spend quality time with their children.

One to One Work

Working on a one to one basis can include a huge variety of options, however before we begin to describe some of the most effective ways of doing this, we need to be mindful of a number of factors.

* It is all too easy to go into a piece of One to One work with our agenda already worked out. Of course we should have a clear idea of the desired outcome for the work, but we should also be listening to fathers, and tailoring our work to respond to not only the need as we have identified it, but also to the need as seen by the father.

* Identifying that need can take time, it is not until a level of trust has been established in the relationship that many of the real issues will come to the fore. Flexibility is the key to much of the success in this kind of work.

* We also need to recognise the limitations of the individual, to do otherwise is to set them up to fail; just as we acknowledge that we ourselves are not "perfect parents", so we should acknowledge that this will apply to the men we are working with. We should constantly be asking whether our expectations are realistic.

* Similarly we also need to acknowledge our own limitations, knowing when to refer on to other specialist agencies can be key to moving families on.

* Often the choice of venue for the work can mean the difference between success and failure. The most obvious choice, the family home, may not always be the most appropriate. Indeed for absent and separated fathers it may well be an impossible choice. Family centres are often seen as an obvious alternative, but be careful as they are sometimes perceived by men as " feminised environments". There are also considerations to be made depending whether we are working with the father on his own, or with his children as well. Parks, beaches, leisure centres etc become an obvious alternative.

* In addition to the 'where', we should also give thought to the 'when'. We are often restricted by the constraints of our own diaries, hours of work, etc. Do not assume that these are the times most convenient for the father. When we disrupt peoples own schedules, and they are sometimes reluctant to admit to this, they are not surprisingly less likely to be focussed on the time they are spending with us. Having one eye on the clock is not the way to bring about meaningful change.

* A safe space and time is the key.
* In all the work we do, especially when working with both fathers and children together, remember that you are the role model. It is nearly always more powerful to actually model the behaviour yourself than to 'preach' about it!
* Workers are often expected to be a mine of information. None of us know everything, but what we must know, is where to access that information. Be honest, and when we "*promise to find out by next week*" , make sure that we do not erode the building trust by not keeping that promise.
* We should also be prepared to act as advocates for fathers (and their children!) in a whole variety of settings. Always be sensitive to literacy levels, and remember environments which we as professionals are comfortable in, may be threatening and hostile to many fathers.
* Probably the most difficult question to answer is that of the timeframe for the work. How long should I consider working with a particular father? I'm afraid that that's a little bit like asking how long is a piece of string? In the end it probably comes down to our own experience and professional judgement (although project managers may take a different view!).

* As mentioned previously this kind of work can often be seen as a prelude to a piece of groupwork; moving people on in this way is often a solution to the last point.

* And finally, the most obvious considerations. We are not there to judge! Be sensitive to ethnic, cultural and religious considerations. The more that we are able to relate to people as individuals then the greater the probability of enhancing their role as parents. The only time that we should be challenging people's personal values, is when they are damaging to the child.

Spending Time Together

There are a number of ways in which we can support and encourage fathers to spend quality time with their children. How you choose to formally structure this work is up to you and the way your organisation works.

It may be that you would choose to set one or more of the following as something a father could attempt in the ensuing days, and then feed back next time you meet. Alternatively there will be times when it is more effective to carry out the activities together, with the worker acting as a role model for the work.

The secret for success, in whichever way you approach it, is that you normalise the behaviour. In other words, it is only when the way a father behaves with his child in a particular way on a routine basis as part of his normal everyday life, that the relationship with the child will be enhanced. Doing something because he has been asked to do so on a particular occasion should only be seen as the beginning.

There are two obvious ways to bring about this transition, firstly be generous with your praise for the father. Praise is an extremely powerful tool, never underestimate it.

And secondly by highlighting the benefits to both the child and the father child relationship. Remember, fathers are far more likely to do something if they see it as something which they are doing for the child and not themselves.

Chapter Six:
Practice

Play

Play is probably the best way of learning, play is vital in the development of a well adjusted and happy child. A child who knows how to play and is able to spend time playing is a joy to be around. Most of the professionals involved in care work know this to be true, and assume that the parents and carers they are dealing with also know this to be true. Unfortunately, this is often not the case. So many parents complain about their children being bored, about them nagging, often the solution to this is that the child doesn't know how to play, hasn't been taught how to play. The parents haven't spent enough time playing with their children, and often they (the parents) are the ones who don't know how to play.

The care professionals need to work with these parents to encourage them to play, and the fathers can be a key in this area. The father or father figure needs to be encouraged to play with the child, and we should not assume that he knows how to play. All parents want their children to be happy and fulfilled in later life, so the advantages of playing need to be stressed, and support given to any initiatives in this area.

The child will learn a huge amount from playing, this can include:

---

      *   Social skills (i.e. sharing)

      *   Teamwork

      *   Rules

      *   Co-ordination skills

      *   Language skills

      *   Life skills

      *   The way things work

      *   Solutions to problems

Often the father will lack the confidence to involve himself in play, or feel that it is beneath him, somehow it will be embarrassing. The care professional needs to model such activities when there is contact with the whole family.

Many fathers assume that by being in the same room as a child they are playing with them, this is not the case.

They need to be active, participating, enjoying it, and showing the child that such activities are worthy. It is a learning experience.

Fathers need to be encouraged to play with their children at every opportunity, and need to be shown that
there are lots of times and places for play:-

    *   In the family home

    *   In a suitable venue (family centre, etc)

    *   In the community (parks, beaches, play-
grounds, etc)

They also need to know that there are many different types of play:-

Creative

Fathers can make things, on the whole they are good with their hands, and they like to be constructive. When this is a shared activity with their child, it teaches the child a huge amount about the way in which the world is made and constructed.

Magical

Play can be imaginative, not based in reality, but fantastic, such play will be hugely beneficial in later life, it will stimulate imagination and innovation, entrepreneurs use these skills.

Educational

This is a misleading title, play is not about sitting in straight lines and learning mathematical solutions by rote. Play is, however, very educational, and it can teach children many different skills through a subtle and non-disciplined way.

Physical

To play is to be active and to be happy. This promotes fitness, can stimulate laughter and joy, enables the child to breath deeply. All of these activities will benefit the child as they grow up.

All play must be age/stage appropriate, and many parents need to be shown what this means.

Under 2's (babies/young toddlers)
*   Keep it simple, lots of smiles, lots of praise, and appropriate noises
*   Don't stand over them, come down to their level
*   Their attention spans may be short, so don't continue an activity once they have lost interest, start a new one
*   The child needs to initiate as well as you, observe what they are doing, don't impose a game or rules
*   Encourage them to dictate where, when and how the activity develops

School age
*   Play needs to be fun, needs to be seen as a joyful activity, not a chore, they will pick up if you are thinking it is a chore
*   Imaginative and creative activities, such as junk modelling, making dens are vital at this stage of development

*   Story telling by the child should be encouraged and developed, the best way to develop this is to model it yourself

*   Just because you may think you don't have a good voice, doesn't mean that you should impose that on your child when he/she wants to sing

*   Even if you know that what they are suggesting will not work, is too ambitious, don't put them down and discourage, they will learn far more from their own failures than by not experiencing it at all

Teenagers

*   Playing with teenagers needs to take into consideration how they feel about themselves, you need to listen to them and take their views into account

*   As they develop hobbies and interests you will need to support these either by participating yourself, or by taking an interest and wanting to know about it

*   They will want to play with their friends, and not want you involved, that is fine, but you also need to show that you are still able to play and have fun, you are not turning into a fossilized dinosaur!

The father also needs to be made aware of the value of play in terms of role modelling for his children. The father who encourages his son to learn through experience is giving a good example of how to develop, the father who plays vigorous and physical games with his daughter is showing her how to be in future life. There are so many advantages to having a playful father for the child, we know that this is a vital and key area in the development of the child, and any work which promotes and supports this will be of benefit not only to the family, but to the wider community as well.

The Rules of Play

* Set aside time - keep to it
* With younger children - get down to their level
* Don't dominate - allow children freedom
* It's your time which is valuable - not the amount of money spent on props
* Fit in with the child's attention span
* Use play to employ praise and reward
* With more than one child - be seen to be fair
* Don't be afraid of getting dirty
* Playing together offers an opportunity for talking and listening together - always communicate, not necesarily about the game
* Should be age/stage appropriate
* Choose the right time
* You don't have to finish every game

Homework/Schoolwork

*   Research shows a gender bias- Maths/ science for dad, arts/crafts for mum
*   Offers an opportunity to engage with the school
*   The parent learns at the same time
*   Signposts to other adult learning opportunities
*   Think about your own (forgotten) skills

Life's Little Rituals

Fathers can be encouraged to take sole responsibility for any number of these.

Some of the most obvious are: -
* Mealtime
* Bedtime
* Bathtime
* Getting ready for school
* Regular journeys

Make sure that the father has the necessary skills to make whichever of these you decide, happen. Start with something relatively straightforward within the context of that particular family. Go through it step by step in advance. Make sure that everyone knows what is expected of them and is comfortable in fulfilling that.

In two parent families talk to the mother as well to make sure that she is also comfortable with what is happening. These simple routines provide plenty of opportunities for relationships to grow and blossom.

Quiet Times

Fathers don't have to be busy in order to spend quality time with their children. Often it is the quieter moments that children remember when recalling their father.

Obvious examples would be: -
*   Reading a story.
*   Talking to them about the family. Children love tohear about what their relations got up to!
*   Listening to a child read.
*   Having a cuddle. Remember that cuddles with fathers are often very different to those of mothers.
*   Share a favourite TV programme together. Television is fine so long as you talk about what is happening and don't just sit there as mindless zombies.
*   Colouring or drawing together.

Being a Taxi

This is not necessarily about driving a car, although this may well be the case. All our children need to be some-where more often than not!

* Take responsibility for the journey.
* Simply getting them safely to their desti -nation, e.g. visiting friends, going to cubs, cinema etc.
* Supporting them once you get there, e.g. doctor, dentist etc.
* Doing the school run. (also one of Life's Little Rituals)

Talk to them, simply sitting in the car together doesn't do it. Children often find a car a safe place to open up about things (as those of you who have worked in Child Protection can testify).

Household Chores

Mothers generally love this one! There are plenty of simple opportunities for children and their fathers to do stuff together. However be mindful of two things, firstly choose chores which are age / stage appropriate for the child, and secondly think about the Health and Safety implications.

*   Washing the car
*   Clearing leaves in the garden
*   Tidying up
*   Washing / drying up
*   Feeding the pets
*   Walking the dog
*   Taking the rubbish out
*   Hoovering

Especially with younger children these can often be an opportunity to have fun together, don't choose chores which you need to take too seriously. The added benefit is that it also makes the task easier for the father. Again it is an opportunity to talk and praise.

Treats and Activities

There is a danger that fathers often associate this one with things which can be expensive. Although there is nothing wrong with spending money on our children, it is the time we spend together which is the most valuable.

Think about alternatives which do not cost anything (or very little).

*   Trips to the park
*   Going swimming
*   Visit the beach (where one is available)
*   Bike rides
*   Rent a video
*   Playing ball games
*   Picnics
*   Staying up late

These activities are also invaluable as part of a reward system when it comes to behaviour management. There is also the opportunity to introduce children to new activities. Fathers can benefit by introducing their children to those things which interest them. Where there is more than one child, and a significant age gap, be careful that treats are structured in a way that does not leave one child feeling excluded.

Something you may hear often is *"I don't take them any-where because they only argue about it"* . Children will gain from one to one time with their father, do the same with their brother or sister next week.

Try and let children choose what they would like to do in these situations; older children will understand the fi-nancial implications of what they are asking, and younger children often find the simplest things the most satisfy-ing.

In addition to time spent in the above way, there should also be opportunities for the whole family to engage in these kind of activities.   Be careful, it is not only the children who can feel left out, mothers may often share the same reaction!

Chapter Seven:
More Practice

Mentors

Many fathers feel isolated, especially in the first years of a child's development. They are building a relationship with the child and often re-building the relationship with the mother. It is a testing time, and when the grandparents are not present or un-supportive, there is little encouragement and support for them. Within this context all fathers need and would benefit from a mentor, someone who can show that they are not alone, someone in whom they can confide their fears and worries, someone who will be there for them.

Most men find it hard to ask for help, especially if it also means admitting to emotional concerns, and showing that they don't know what they are doing. So, if the father is to receive support it has to be undertaken tactfully and with care, in a way that doesn't alienate or make him feel inadequate. As with most things, someone who has been through the same kinds of experience is always the best guide, but these individuals need training and guidance.

The best way to develop these kinds of support structures would be to consider:-

Recruiting from known fathers -
Those who have already received support and you know will be sympathetic and helpful. To do this work will be new not just for the father receiving, but also for the father who is giving it. You need to be confident that they will able to do the work, and that they know what they are talking about. That they are in favour of play, won't promote smacking or harsh discipline, are able to listen and will encourage the father to confide and express himself.

Either as a voluntary or sessional scheme-
Developed in the ways which best suits the fathers, not worked to a strict regime or schedule. Creating an individual programme which can be appraised and assessed easily.

Are based around personal development-
Such mentoring will not only focus on the father and his child, they will have to deal with issues around the relationship with the mother, and possibly issues with the extended family. This can also lead to involvement and strategies for an individual to seek to re-gain employment, personal issues around self-worth and value.

Training issues

These kinds of mentoring programmes need to be supervised and maintained well. They will call for specialised training schemes, and will inevitably develop a wide range of issues and concerns within the family as well as within those who are mentoring.

Can support the professional

Such schemes are invaluable in providing support to the family and child, and when run well will also ease the workload of the professionals involved with the family.

This may affect male recruitment issues

A successful scheme with mentors receiving training and a wide range of experience will supply suitable candidates for jobs within the caring services.

Whole Family

Ideally there should not be the need for separate courses for fathers. The support which comes naturally between a mother and a father should be sufficient, and this can be developed with the help of the extended family. Unfortunately, this is often not the case. Many families don't have a father figure, many fathers feel inadequate and challenged by fatherhood, and many fathers are now absent and ignore their responsibilities.

Where the father is present, or a father figure has been created, the support from the care professionals needs to be very creative and generous. As we have seen such families are fragile, they need encouragement and praise to continue. There is a need for preventative support for existing couples, which will prevent the break-ups of the future. All too often the support and care is given once the father has left, the crisis has happened, and it is too late to retain that original shape and form for the family.

This support needs to be in a wide range of forms, in-cluding:-

Existing service users

Where a family is a service user, to identify the needs and concerns of the father and to ensure that he is sup-ported and praised. All too often his role is ignored and sidelined, and the care professionals need to ensure that he is seen to be rewarded with praise when he takes responsibility for changing nappies, or taking the children off for a day, etc.

Bring father into process

When discussions and decisions are being made he needs to be part of the process, or at least feel he can have a say, and will be listened to. Also the care profes-sionals need to talk to the mother and the father as a unit rather than just focusing on the mother. They need to choose times when the father is around.

Provides consistency in parenting

By doing the above the father will be encouraged to take his role in the family more seriously. He will be encour-aged to be actively involved in the upbringing of his child. This will support the mother, it will encourage her to trust him with the children, and to develop an equal and shar-ing role within the family.

Overcome some of the gender stereotyping

Whilst the father feels rightly or wrongly that he is being excluded from the task at hand, he can also continue to not involve himself with the child. He can perpetuate an indolent and un-supportive male role model, which will frustrate and cause friction within the family.

Discrimination

Many men feel they are discriminated against whilst being a father, and the professionals need to be able to support the fathers as they seek to develop their relationships with the children and the mother. It doesn't help if the professionals also perpetuate gender stereotypes and roles within the family - expecting the dad to go out and get the job, expecting him not to be able to look after the children.

Bringing Dads Together

It is widely acknowledged that there is a huge benefit to having Mother and Toddler groups. They are promoted and developed all over Britain, and have become a feature of just about every community. Not only do the mothers gain a great deal of support and encouragement at these centres, but there are also obvious benefits for the children and the families involved.

By contrast fathers are expected to be able to cope with family life without such support, and to an extent that functions well. However, with the changing roles being undertaken by men and women; increasing numbers of women working; life style changes; the development of more flexible working regimes; and changes to maternity and paternity leave.

Not all fathers want to meet other fathers, many feel they are fine as they are, and they associate such behaviour as being weak or soft. However, increasing numbers are prepared to explore a more rational response, and this can be promoted in a wide range of ways within a community. This is a relatively new development, and as such is still in the experimental stages. There is no one way to go about setting such support structures up, each community will have it's particular issues, and there is no one formula which works every time. However, there are some basic guidelines we can give:-

Small informal groups
To expect lots of fathers to turn up, and to continue to turn up week after week is not realistic. Such groups start with a core and can develop given time and the right support. However, they can also fall apart for no apparent reason, so they always need nurturing and support.

Shared problems/issues
The fathers need to be able to feel safe, to recognise each other as being similar and equals. They need to know that they are being supported and facilitated in whatever way is necessary. Once that is established they will be sharing their problems and issues with each other, and seeking assistance from the professionals.

Support each other - outside of service
When these groups work well the fathers will continue the contact outside of the group, and develop strong bonds of support and mutual help. This is to be encouraged and promoted as it will ease the workload of the professionals involved.

Normalise the role

Such groups enable the fathers to realise that they are doing a good job, that others are struggling just as hard as they, and that they are normal. When this happens they can then be encouraged to become more adventurous with their children, and encourage each other to play, to be creative with their children.

Share expertise/skills

The group need to be able to share their own skills and expertise, this will create ownership not only of those particular sessions, but of the group as a whole. They will learn from each other and this can be of benefit to the children and the wider community as well.

Can be task led group

The group can take on issues and undertake projects within the wider community, and this leads to a great sense of achievement and pride within the fathers. In addition this can lead to a wider publicising of the group. When this occurs the children gain a great deal of pride in their fathers, and this can be very beneficial to the family.

Separated Fathers

The circumstances for this group of fathers are by definition different. The United Nations Convention *(Article 9)* states that all children have a right to a meaningful relationship with BOTH parents. Because this is not always easy we need to make extra efforts to facilitate it *(Bainham et al. 2003)*. If extra motivation were needed, just look at the high rates of children who lose contact with the non-resident parent, usually the father, within the first two years after separation.

On the positive side, when separated fathers do have contact, it is generally with the expectation at least that it will be quality time. Unfortunately there are often a number of barriers which preclude this from happening.

Some of these are: -
   * Housing issues (small flats and bedsits)
   * Geographical issues (distance from the child)
   * Ongoing problems with the ex-partner
   * Lack of suitable affordable venues
   * Court proceedings, CSA etc.

Many of these fathers will only see their children at evenings and weekends, not generally part of professionals normal working hours. This is a problem that can only be resolved at project level.

Mothers often want fathers to be more involved in their children's lives, but on 'their own terms', so retaining control. Mothers are most likely to act in this way, as gatekeepers to parenting, when they are not resident with the child's father.

Teachers are often nervous, and fear possible aggression or child abuse from non-resident fathers. They are also often fearful of alienating and upsetting mothers.

Separated fathers often report that the biggest problem facing them is where to take the child. Even when finances allow them to take the child out, there still remainslittle opportunity for any kind of private time together. Added to this, the child will eventually get fed up with going to a famous burger chain all the time.

When the child does not associate seeing their father with an enjoyable experience then that is the time they start telling their mother the "don't want to see daddy on Saturday", and the beginning of the end of the relationship. No one is particularly to blame, but the outcome for both father and child is disastrous

How we can seek to overcome these difficulties: -

* Family Centres that are open at weekends (some already do).
* Allowing fathers to support each other (groups like Gingerbread, Families Need Fathers)
* Offering fathers positive alternatives to the obvious ones (see above).
* Advocating on their behalf for more suitable housing.
* Lobbying for a fairer system (schools etc).

Chapter Eight:
Conclusions

Conclusions

Fathers are often the missing link in services designed to provide better outcomes for children. Where support has proved to be effective it has generally involved looking at the wider picture of the way families operate, and this must include the father figure if there is one. We recognise that families may struggle on a number of levels, economic, social, emotional etc etc. Yet conventional thinking has only thought of fathers as contributing at the economic level, i.e. as the breadwinner. The growing body of research over the last ten years has clearly demonstrated the benefits to children in particular, and families as a whole, when the father figure is involved in all aspects of the family dynamic. Families are not static institutions, they evolve over time and the skill levels of the individuals within the family must also evolve to meet these changing needs.

The latest generation of fathers have taken this change on board and are now behaving responsibly towards their children - they are playing with them, they are spending time with them, and seeking to participate fully, or as fully as they can, in the upbringing and decision making. This kind of active participation was frowned upon just 20 years ago, indeed, it is still seen as 'soft' by some people today. This level of participation needs to be encouraged and built upon in the future, and we need to oppose those who see such behaviour as being weak or not of value. The effect of such participation is immeasurable, and as a culture and society we need to acknowledge and encourage it.

Women's participation in the labour market has increased *(O'Brien. 2004)*, and the impacts of this on family life are today only too evident. Concomitant with the financial benefits this may confer on families however are the additional strains placed on childcare. Increasingly we see grandparents taking on roles which a generation ago would not have been thought necessary.   It is important therefore that we see our work with fathers within this wider context.   The love and care which a father can give his children, added to the love and care from the mother and grandparents, will in many ways create a more balanced child. Indeed the attention a child receives from it's father is different and special, it is a unique gift, which can often be life transforming and very significant in the child's development.

The fact that we (Fatherskills) see children at the centre of working with fathers does not however mean that we cannot recognise the wider benefits that this work may bring. Children suffer, often inadvertently, in families where there are high levels of stress on whatever level, and looking for solutions in isolation is often not the best way forward. In a 'perfect world' we should not have to separate fathers from the wider parenting agenda, their role, on all levels, should be taken as read. We make no apologies for the fact that we appear to be talking ourselves out of a job, as this has to be our eventual goal. In the meantime, and for the many reasons that we have looked at in the preceding pages, this is not the case. Many fathers today need to be seen, not only as a hard to reach group, but as a special case, i.e. they have a lot of catching up to do in order not only to fulfil their own potentials *(Palkovitz. 2002)*, but those of their children and families as a whole. These fathers need to be encouraged, shown how to play with their children, as well as praised for giving time to their children when they do.

We have been working in Wales for over 30 years, with families, with fathers and mothers, children and in a wide range of settings. During this time it has become clear that many of the so-called 'deprived' families are actually giving a huge amount of love, time and care to their children. This has proved quite sufficient to create and nurture well-balanced and respectable members of society. Despite the lack of money, and the consequent lack of access to the best toys or latest gadgets, these children are fine. All too often parents see their financial and monetary contribution to their child's upbringing as being of paramount value. It is not - it is the time, care and love you give the child which is important. How much you listen to your children and how often you praise and acknowledge them which has the longer lasting effect. We come across many families who outwardly seem to be 'providing' for their children, in fact, they are behaving extremely childishly and immaturely towards them. The consequences of their actions can be seen in criminal behaviour, drug addiction, and other anti-social traits within their children as they grow up.

Another recent phenomenon is the increasing number of parents who believe that it is it the teachers responsibility to education their children in all aspects of values and behaviour. This negation of responsibility again reflects a lack of maturity and an inability to fully grasp the consequences of being a parent. This leads to an increasingly passive attitude towards society, a lack of community involvement and no sense of pride, ownership or place. We all acknowledge that these are major problems in society today, but how we address and change them is still controversial. Some of the media has taken a very simplistic view of these problems and presented them as a consequence of the liberated and liberal past. We do not hold with this, and feel that a more mature and sensible look at the problems can reveal more effective ways of changing society.

This links into the two schools of thought that prevail today when it comes to parenting.

On the one hand there are the didactic parenting programmes, simple instructions which offer appropriate responses often specific to particular behaviours and needs. Being instructed and passively accepting a 'truth', which may or may not be appropriate.

On the other hand are programmes which emphasise the relationship between parent and child. This is not a 'soft' option, it asks that we take responsibility for our actions and start to understand the complexity of parenting.

When the relationship between the father (or mother) is based on sound foundations there should be no need for prescriptive formulas about how to best respond to any given situation, they will take care of themselves. If this sounds oversimplistic, PLEASE TRY IT! What this does not mean however is that these relationships are easy, they are not, and often require lots of effort from both parties. We take this as read when it comes to the relationship with our partners but often seem to think that these rules don't apply to our children. It is only when our children reach their teenage years that we start to realise that we may have to start compromising.

If there are two things we need to remember about relationships, they are these:-

· Relationship problems are ALWAYS caused by both parties
· You can't always control the other persons behaviour, but you can control your own

Nobody is suggesting here that we should be constantly giving in to every whim and ignoring every little peccadillo, what it is suggesting is that we need to give our children some respect. Children who are shown respect quickly learn to respect others, including us, their parents! Inherent within this approach is also the fact that it allows space for the nature of the relationship to develop and grow. The dangers of ignoring (neglecting) our children's needs are just as bad as indulging (spoiling) them. We would not realistically expect an adult relationship to survive under these conditions, but seem to see no contradictions when it comes to our children. Just as we have rules and boundaries in place for adult relationships, so should these be in place for children and young people. They define what we consider acceptable and we instinctively recognise that if we step outside them there will be consequences. These are important life skills for our children to learn, and they will carry the benefits of them long after they have left our care and attentions.

The two of us are commited to this work, we have specialised in working with children, men and fathers, for many years now. Not many people seek out such work, far less actually want to do it. However, both of us can categorically state that it is a privilege to do such work. The men with whom we work are a constant delight, surprise, challenge and worry, and that represents the kind of work we want to undertake! Most people who work in the caring professions, or who work with children, almost invariably focus their attention on the mothers, and those father figures who are present can often feel invisible and unheard. We feel this is a hugely missed opportunity, we know it is additional work, but we also know that it will be of benefit to the children. The great majority of fathers we work with love and care hugely for their children, they may express and show it in ways which women find hard to fathom, but they do. We know that some fathers are abusive, violent and untrustworthy, but that doesn't mean that all fathers are like that. Please keep this in mind when working with families, mothers and children in the future.

We know that many of fathers who have committed themselves to their children have done so because they want their children to have a better experience than they had. These fathers are aware of the general lack of love, expression, and emotion by the previous generation, and are seeking to improve this situation. Many don't know how to do this, but with help they can see that by playing, by spending time, by expressing emotions, love and care, they will be of benefit to their children. This benefit will spread like the ripples on a pond. It will increase the father's confidence - a father who knows he is doing a good job, will be a positive role model and will have more self-esteem. A child who receives such attention from their father will be very self confident, assured, able to communicate and a good contributor to society. This will affect girls in a wide range of ways, which will include - their choices in terms of their future partners, they will want someone who is able to express themselves. The boys will be affected similarly:- they will also be more able to talk and discuss their emotions with other people. The mothers will be affected by this in turn, they will be able to trust men, they will ask for support and receive it. The ripples from the increasingly confident family unit, will affect grand parents, aunts and uncles, as a positive role model is seen and experienced. This will affect the wider community increasing community awareness and pride.

So, for us, this work is not just about fathers, it is about the wider community, and the kind of future we want to build as a society. By enabling and encouraging participation and confident parenting skills in fathers, we are making a significant and important impact on their children's lives, and, in turn, future children's lives.

REFERENCES

* **Allen, J. & Hawkins, A.** (1999) *Maternal Gatekeeping: Mothers beliefs and behaviours that inhibit greater father involvement in family work.* Journal of Marriage and the Family. **60**, 809-820

* **Bainham, A, et al.** (2003) *Children and their Families: contact, rights and Welfare.* Oxford-Portland, Oregon: Hart Publishing.

* **Beail, N. & McGuire** (1997) (Eds) *Fathers Psychological Perspectives.* London

* **Bertaux, D. & Delcroix, C.** (1992) *Where have all the daddies gone?* In U. Bjornberg (Ed) *Eoropean Parents in the 1990's.* New Brunswick: Transaction Publishers.

* **Collingwood Bakeo, A, & Clarke, L.** (2004) *Child population in 'The Health of Children & Young People'* London: The stationery Office.

*   **Desforges, C. & Abouchaar, A.** (2003) The Impact of Parental Involvement, Parental Support, and Family Education on Public Achievement and Adjustment: A literature review. *DfES Research report 433.* London: DfES

*   **Dunn, J. et al.** (2000) *Parents' and partners' life course and family experience:* Journal of Child Psychology and Psychiatry, **41**, 955-968

*   **EOC** (2003) *Fathers: Balancing work and family.* Manchester: Equal Opportunities Commission.

*   **Flouri, E. & Buchanan, A.** (2002) *What predicts good relationships with parents in adolescence, and partners in adult life:* Journal of Family Psychology. **16**, 186-198.

*   **Flouri, E. & Buchanan, A.** (2003) *What predicts fathers involvement in their children?* British Journal of Developmental Psychology, **21**, 81-98

* **Ghate, D. & Ramella, M.** (2002) *Positive Parenting. National Evaluation of the Youth Justice Board's Parenting programme.* Policy Research Bureau for Youth Justice Board.

* **Ghate, D. Shaw, C, & Hazel, N.** (2000) *Fathers and family centres: engaging fathers in preventative services.* Joseph Rowntree Foundation.

* **Goldman, R.** (2005) *Fathers' Involvement in their Children's Education.* National Family & Parenting Institute: London

* **Henwood, K. & Procter, J.** (2003) *The good father: reading men's accounts of paternal involvement during the transition to first time fatherhood.* British Journal of Social Psychology **42**, (3) 335-337

* **Heubeck, B. et al** (1986) *Father Involvement and Responsibility in Family Therapy.* In M.E.Lamb (Ed). *The fathers Role: Applied Perspectives.* New York: Wiley

* **Jaffee, S. R. et al** (2003) *Life with (or without) father:* Child development , **74**, 109-126.

*   **Lamb, M.** (1997) *The Role of the Father in child development.* New York. John Wiley & Sons.

*   **Lamb, M. and Tamis-Lemonda, C.** (2004) The Role of the Father: An Introduction. In M. Lamb (Ed) *The Role of the father in Child development,* 4th Edition. New Jersey: John Wiley & Sons.

*   **Lewis, C.** (1997) *Fathers and Preschoolers. In M.E. Lamb (Ed) The role of father in child development.* New York: Wiley.

*   **Lewis, C.** (2000) *A mans place in the home: Fathers & families in the UK.* York: Joseph Rowntree Foundation.

*   **Marsiglio, W. et al.** (2000) *Scholarship on fatherhood in the 1990's and beyond.* Journal of Marriage and the Family, **62**, 1173-1191

*   **Motluk, A.** (2000) *Father Instincts* Orgyn, **4**: 24-27

*   **O'Brien, M.** (2004) *Fathers and Family Support.* National Family & Parenting Institute: London

*   **O'Brien, M.** (2004) *Shared caring: bringing fathers into the frame.* Manchester: Equal Opportunities Commission.

*   **O'Brien, M. & Shemilt, I.** (2003) Working fathers: earning & caring. Manchester: EOC

*   **Palkovitz, R.** (2002) *Involved fathering in men's adult development: provisional balances.* New Jersey: Lawrence Erlbaum Associates.

*   **Pleck, J. H. & Mascaidrelli, B. P.** (2004) Parental Involvement by U.S. Residential Fathers: Levels, sources & consequences. In M. Lamb (Ed) *The role of the father in Child development* (4thEdition) New jersey; John Wiley & Sons

*   **PRB.** (2004) *Parenting in Poor Environments:* In (Ed) D. Ghate & Hazel. Policy Research Bureau: London.

*   **Scott, J.** (2004) *Family, gender and educational attainment in Britain: a longitudinal study.* Journal of Comparative family Studies **35**, (4)

*   **Storey, A.** (2000) *Evolution & Human Behaviour,* vol **21**, p79.

- **Whelan, A. & Lupton, P.** (1998) *Promoting successful breastfeeding among women with a low income.* Midwifery, **14**, 94-100.
- **United Nations Convention on the Rights of the Child.** Ratified by the UK Government 16th December 1991.

TONY IVENS

Tony comes originally from a science backgroung,but has been working in the parenting field in Wales for a number of years, during which time he has worked for both the statutory and voluntary sectors. He has always had a special interest in working with fathers and was responsible for much of the pioneering work with fathers in Wales.

In addition to this work he collaborated on the development of Living With Teenagers, and co-authored the One to One support programme for Carmarthenshire.

 He currently has responsibility for the Fatherhood Wales Forum, the All Wales network for professionals working with fathers. During the last few years he has shared these experiences through the delivery of training programmes to hundreds of workers from a variety of disciplines.

More recently Tony was a member of the Welsh Assembly Government Working Group which drew up the Parenting Action Plan for Wales.

He is currently married with two grown up children.

NICK CLEMENTS

Nick trained in film making, performance art and social work. In 1981 he set up The Pioneers Community Arts Team and managed them until 2002, providing employment for over 80 people, using the arts and creativity in some of the poorest communities throughout Wales, Europe, America and Asia.

Throughout that time he always tended to work with boys and men, naturally gravitating to them, and enabling them to deal with their issues through creativity.

He has run training programmes and workshops for men and fathers for over 12 years, specialising in creativity, economic and social impact, and personal development. As well as delivering such programmes for care professionals.

Nick is a well known author of community arts books, and makes documentary films about father's issues.

He is the father of two children.

FATHERSKILLS CONSULTANCY AND TRAINING

Consultancy

Fatherskills offers a range of expert consultancy services to meet the needs of your project. We can advise on making your service father friendly, mentoring and the use of volunteers, evaluation, staff development and training needs.

Working With Fathers

An intensive two day training course which will introduce participants to the ethos of working with fathers. The principles explored in this book are developed into exercises and group discussions. Some of the barriers and difficulties to working with fathers are explained, and solutions offered. By the end of the two days the participants will have the necessary skills and confidence to engage in meaningful work with fathers.

Living With Teenagers

An intensive two day training course which will provide participants with the necessary skills to deliver the Living With Teenagers programme. Participants will be introduced to the basics of groupwork theory and the logistics of setting up a group. They will experience at first hand many of the exercises used during the delivery of the programme. Included in the training is the Living With Teenagers manual, providing details of all the sessions along with useful tips on their delivery.

New Horizons

A one day training course introducing participants to the principles of working with men, the specific issues surrounding gaining access to them. They will experience at first hand many useful exercises to be used with men to encourage them to open up. The training will enable participants to develop this important part of their work delivery.

Workshops

We offer 2hr taster workshops on all three of the above programmes.